Shari Lewis

presents

101

Things

for Kids to Do

Library of Congress Cataloging-in-Publication Data:
Lewis, Shari. Shari Lewis presents 101 things for kids to do.
SUMMARY: Presents 101 tricks, stunts, and simple crafts,
including explanations of how to turn a quarter into
a dime and make a drinking cup from a piece of paper.
1. Creative activities and seat work—Juvenile literature.
2. Tricks—Juvenile literature. [1. Tricks.   2. Magic tricks.
3. Amusements.   4. Handicraft]   I. Buller, Jon, ill.   II. Title.
III. Title: 101 things for kids to do.   IV. Title: Shari Lewis
presents one hundred one things for kids to do.   V. Title: One
hundred one things for kids to do.   VI. Title: One hundred and one things
for kids to do.   GV1203.L4748   1987   793.8   86-43065
ISBN: 0-394-88966-5 (trade); 0-394-98966-X (lib. bdg.)

Manufactured in the United States of America   2   3   4   5   6   7   8   9   0

Shari Lewis

presents

101 Things for Kids to Do

illustrated by Jon Buller

Random House 🏠 New York

Contents

Introduction

I love to know how to do things that nobody else can do. If you're like me, then you'll find lots of fun in *101.*

This is a book full of secrets. Some are "betchas"—pranks that only *you* can pull, because only you know that special little something that makes them work. You'll also find puppets and toys to make, brainteasers, games to play, and magic tricks that will amaze your friends.

Here's how to get the most fun out of this book:

1. Use it just the way you use a menu in a restaurant. Pick and choose what you like best.

2. Remember that instructions are like recipes. Most work easily if you follow directions. For others, you have to get the "feel" of them. Then they work like a dream.

Some, like Fish Spinner on page 9, are sweet and simple. Others, like The Wandering Water Trick on page 27, are a little . . . well, trickier. But they're worth it. You'll feel proud of yourself when you get the hang of 'em.

3. If you don't understand one part of an instruction, just read on. Usually, by the time you're done, it will all make sense.

4. Before you do a stunt or a trick or a puppet or *anything* for anybody else, do it for the mirror. Next, do it for the dog. Or for your kid brother. By then you'll be a pro at doing the funny trick or stunt, and it'll work every time.

Did you hear the joke about the magician who called the girl onstage to be his assistant? To prove to the audience that this girl was not his stooge, the magician asked, "Now, you've never seen me before, have you?" And the little girl answered, "No, Daddy."

That's the story of my life. My father was the Official Magician for the City of New York. His stage name was Peter Pan the Magic Man. Ever since I can remember, my father pulled rabbits out of hats and made coins drop out of my friends' ears. He showed me most of the goodies on these pages. That's how *I* know them. In this book, I'll show them to you, and *you'll* know them too.

Shari Lewis

1 The Unpoppable Balloon

I'd like to start off this book with a bang. The thing is, with this trick there isn't one!

You will need a balloon, a piece of cellophane tape, and a pin. Blow up the balloon. Put the piece of tape on it, anywhere. Hold the balloon so that the tape is facing *you*. Show the pin to your audience. Ask them if they're ready for the big bang. Then boldly stick the pin through the tape into the balloon and, keeping hold of the pin, remove it from the balloon. Your friends will expect the balloon to pop — but it won't!

2 Square Deal

You hand a square piece of paper to a pal and say, "If you can tear it into four equal pieces, I'll give you a quarter."

Now, tearing a square into four equal pieces is not hard. After your pal does it and demands to be paid, you reply, "Yes, you did it. Here's your quarter." And as you say that, you hand your friend one of the four pieces of paper. It's a quarter, after all—a quarter of the square of paper!

3 The Dancing Pencils

I've done silly things in my time, but this is the silliest. However, whenever I show it to anybody, they do it again and again and again!

Take two pencils of the same length. Wind a thick rubber band around them loosely (picture 1). Now twist the pencils in opposite directions, winding up the rubber band. Do it until you can't wind the rubber band anymore (picture 2).

Now hold the pencils about an inch above the floor and let go. Watch 'em dance (picture 3).

FRISKY, AREN'T THEY?

4 The Great Train Connection

Cut a strip of paper about 1 inch wide and about 12 inches long.

Bring one small end of the paper around in front until it meets the strip just past the center. Hold it there with a paper clip (picture 1). Now bring the other end around the back of the strip. Hold it in that position with another paper clip (picture 2).

Now, as you bend the paper and put on the paper clips you say:

"Ever wonder how railway cars link up? They come from distant places along the tracks. The tracks wind this way and that." Bend the paper. "One car is on this track." Slip on the first clip. "And another car is on that track." Bend the paper and put the second clip in place. Next, grasp one little end of the paper firmly in one hand, the other little end in the other hand (picture 3). Quickly pull the ends in opposite directions, and as the strip straightens, the two clips will fly in the air joined together (picture 4). As you pull say: "The train cars get closer and closer and when they meet . . . they link up!" And so they do!

HINT, HINT: Every once in a while the paper clips *don't* link up. I don't know why. It's all in knowing how hard and how fast to pull the ends of the strip. Practice it once or twice for the dog, until it feels right. And if it doesn't work the first time you do it for an audience, don't panic. Set it up and do it again. It's worth it! Just remember to stand far enough away from your audience so they don't get zapped by the clips.

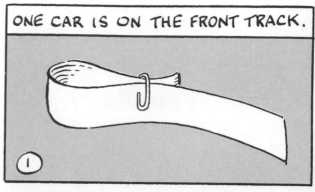
ONE CAR IS ON THE FRONT TRACK.

ANOTHER CAR IS ON THE BACK TRACK.

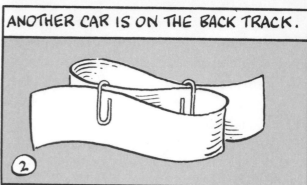
THE CARS GET CLOSER AND CLOSER...

AND WHEN THEY MEET...

THEY LINK UP!

5 Foiled Again

Here's a ball game your folks might even let you play in the house, since there's no big hard ball to bang into anything.

One person becomes the pitcher and pitches little balls (either wadded-up balls of aluminum foil or Ping-Pong balls). The catcher holds two paper cups (the bigger the better), one in each hand.

The only way the catcher can catch the ball is by clapping the two cups together around the ball. For every catch, the catcher gets a point. If the catcher misses, the catcher becomes the pitcher, and the player who was the pitcher takes the two cups, one in each hand, and becomes the new catcher. See who gets to ten first.

I GOT IT!

6 1000—the Hard Way

Betcha can't write the number 1000 without lifting your pencil from the paper or connecting the numbers. Give up?

HERE'S HOW: Fold down a flap at the top of a sheet of paper. Write the number 1 so that it extends past the edge. Without lifting your pencil, continue the line up onto the flap for a loop. That will become the first 0. Do the same for the next two 0's. Then lift the flap, and you'll have done it—written the number 1000 without lifting your pencil from the paper or connecting the numbers!

7 Dot's a Circle

Can you draw a circle with a dot in the center of it without lifting your pen? Yes, of course you can, or I wouldn't have brought it up!

HERE'S HOW: Fold up one of the lower corners of a piece of paper so that it forms a flap (see picture 1). Right past the point of that flap—*but not on it*—draw a dot (picture 2). Then, without lifting your pen from the paper, draw a line from that dot *down onto the corner flap and around to the top edge of the flap* (picture 3). When you reach the edge of the flap, start drawing a circle around the dot until you hit the other edge of the flap.

Careful now! Don't lift your pen. Lift the flap and complete the circle (see picture 4).

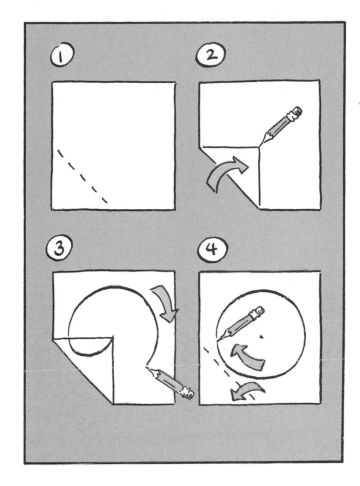

8 A Hole in Your Hand

This is an optical illusion.

Roll a piece of paper into a rather thin tube.

Hold the tube up to one eye, but keep the other eye open as well. Place your other hand (the one that's not holding the tube) with the palm facing you, so that the side of the hand is touching the tube. (Remember: Both eyes are open.) Look through the tube and move a hand toward you and away from you until the hole suddenly seems to be in the center of your hand—in fact, it looks like you're staring right through a hole in your hand.

9 Paper Drinking Cup

This drinking cup, which takes just a second to make out of a piece of notebook or typing paper, *really* holds water!

You can make a big cup or a teeny one, depending on the size of your paper.

Start with a square. Place it on the table so one point is aimed directly at you (picture 1). Bring that bottom point up to meet the top point so it forms a triangle (picture 2). Sharpen the crease at the bottom of the triangle (picture 3).

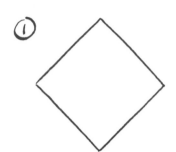
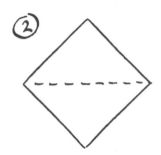
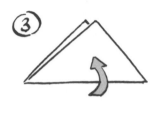

Pick up the corner on the right side of the triangle and bring that corner over to the other side until it touches the middle of the left side (pictures 4 and 5). Sharpen your fold. Bring the other corner (the one on the left side) across until it touches the middle of the right side.

Now your paper looks like it has its arms folded (picture 6).

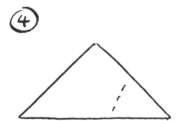
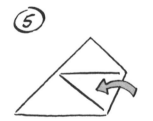

There are two loose flaps on top. Bend down the top one toward you. Sharpen the crease. Turn the cup around. Now bring the other flap toward you, sharpen the crease, and you've done it (see picture 7).

Hold the cup with the mouth on top, pop it open, and pour in your drink.

10 Fish Spinner

This flying fish is a super spinner.

Cut a skinny strip of paper about 7 inches long and ¾ of an inch wide.

Near the top, cut a slit on the right side of the strip. Be sure to cut only halfway across the paper. Near the bottom, cut another slit, this time on the left side. This slit should only go halfway across the paper too.

Curve the strip of paper around so that the bottom slit meets the top slit. Fit the slits into each other.

Now throw your flying fish high up in the air, and it will whirl and twirl all the way to the ground.

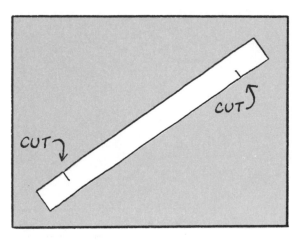

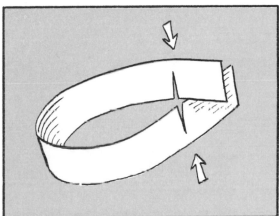

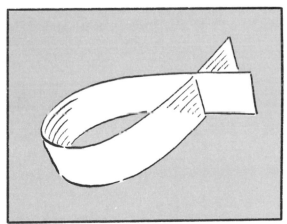

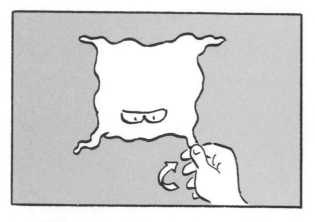

11 Napkin Bug

Here's how you can make a crazy critter that will scuttle around your dining table in a very peculiar manner.

Twist the four corners of a paper napkin to look like legs. Then, with a felt-tipped pen, draw fierce eyes. Now put a lemon or orange under the napkin so the four "legs" just touch the table.

Poke this buggy thing with your finger. It'll squirm this way and that as it changes directions. It'll look as though it can't decide whether to escape or attack!

12 Catchy Coins

This juggling stunt will really impress your friends, and it's easy enough so that you'll get the hang of it after practicing for only a short while.

Holding your hand palm up, place a little pile of coins on your elbow. Cup your hand so that it forms a little pocket aimed at your elbow. Now drop your elbow (suddenly and with a smooth circular swing of your arm). This will bring your hand to just below where your elbow was, and you'll catch the pile of coins.

The real secret is not to throw the coins either up or out. Just sweep your hand down and drop your elbow quickly out from under the coins. Your hand will simply be where the coins are. If you haven't gotten it by the second try, bend your knees a little as you do the stunt.

It probably won't work the first time, but stick with it—you'll soon be able to catch the coins neatly and cleanly.

13 The Magic Pen

You may not have a magic wand, but you do have a "magic pen" that's just as nifty.

Show your friends that your hand is empty. Put your "magic pen" in your empty hand and make a fist. Tap the top of the pen with your other hand, pushing the pen out through the bottom of your fist.

Then tap your closed fist with the "magic pen" just as if it were a magic wand. And when you open your hand—presto!—there's a dime.

HERE'S HOW: Start with a pen that has a prong for clipping onto a pocket. Secretly wedge a dime under the prong of your pen. Now hold the pen upside down so that the prong is at the bottom. Make sure the dime can't be seen—the picture shows you how to cover it with just two fingers. Place the pen (still upside down) into your other fist. Hold it tightly. Now tap or push the top of the pen so it slides down through your fist and out the other side. As you do this, the dime will be pushed off the prong into your closed fist. Now turn your fist so the fingers are facing down and tap the back of the fist with your magic pen. And when you open that fist, I wouldn't be at all surprised if you've made a dime appear in it.

14 The Magic Penny

Here's a clever trick that'll startle your friends, and all you need are a couple of pennies and a quarter. (Actually, a half dollar is better, but harder to come by!)

HERE IS WHAT YOUR AUDIENCE SEES: On your open palm there is a penny on top of a quarter. With your other hand you pick up the penny and drop it into your pocket. At the same time, you close the hand with the quarter in it. When you open your fist, there's the penny again in your right hand, right on top of the quarter!

HERE'S HOW: Place one penny so that it's hidden under the quarter. Then place the other penny on *top* of the quarter. Put them on your palm as shown in the picture.

Now pick up that top penny and drop it into your pocket. At the same time, curl the fingers holding the hidden penny and quarter (to make sure they don't clank) and then close that hand into a fist. (This will turn the two coins upside down. Now the penny will be on top.)

Ask your friends, "Where do you think the penny is?" Your pals will say, "In your pocket."

At this point, open your hand. "Nope," you say, "the penny's still here in my hand!" And as your friends are examining the coins you can quietly whisper, "Thank you, Mr. Washington, thank you, Mr. Lincoln."

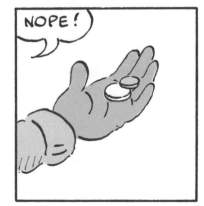

15 Your Dinky Pinky

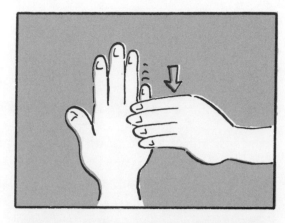

Would you like to shrink your pinky? No, wait—I take that question back because you're sure to say no. Let me put it this way. Once you see how silly it looks to shrink your pinky, I bet you'll want to do it for all your friends.

They'll see you hold your left hand in front of you, fingers pointing straight up. With your other hand, you'll grab that left pinky, and suddenly it'll seem to grow smaller and smaller.

HERE'S HOW: Hold your left hand, palm facing you. Grasp the left pinky at the top knuckle. Pinch it between the thumb and pointer finger of your right hand. Keep the rest of the fingers of your right hand together (see picture). Now press straight down on the pinky. Your little finger will bend, of course. But no one will see that, because most of the pinky will be hidden behind the fingers of your right hand.

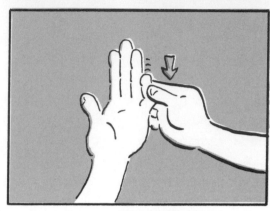

As the pinky bends, don't let the tip lean in toward the palm. Keep that tip pointing straight up.

Try it in front of a mirror first, and then show the world what a weird thing you can do!

THAT IS WEIRD!

14

16 Ten, Minus One!

Fingers were made to count on. Right? Here's a finger stunt you can count on to bewilder your friends!

Clasp your fingers together and have a friend count them! Ten fingers, right? Next, turn your back on your friend, and mutter those amazing magic words. (I don't know which magic words work for you, but whatever they are, if they work, that's amazing!)

Then turn back to your friend and say, "Now count my fingers." And your friend will find that—although your hands look normal—you have made one finger disappear!

HERE'S HOW: The second time you clasp your hands, stick your middle finger underneath so it's resting on your palm. It won't show from the front! Ask your pals to point to each finger as they count—they won't believe it as they see and *feel* that you've only got nine!

17 The Finger Fake-Out

Here's a stunt that will really have you all mixed up: Hold your arms down in front of you. Cross your wrists and clasp all of your fingers together. Bring your hands in toward your body. Then bring them up by bending your elbows until your hands are near your chest, fingers on top.

HERE'S THE MIXED-UP PART OF THIS STUNT: You'll now find that you are so confused about where your fingers are, you won't be able to move them. Don't believe me? Okay. Ask someone to point to any one of your fingers *without touching it.* Now you try to move that finger. No luck, right?

This is all the more amazing when you consider that you've had that finger with you all of your life!

18 An All-time First

This trick will drive your pals nuts! Say to someone: "I can show you something that you never saw, that I never saw, that nobody ever saw. And after both of us have seen it, nobody will see it again."

Then get a peanut, crack open the shell, and take out the nut. Neither of you ever saw it before, nor did anyone else. Next, pop the nut into your mouth and eat it. Nobody will ever see it again!

YOU WILL NOW SEE WHAT HAS NEVER BEEN SEEN BEFORE...

19 Six-Card Lift

Can you arrange six cards so that all six cards can be lifted up by picking up just *one* card by the edges? The cards *cannot* be placed one under another—that's too easy!

The solution is tricky, but if you arrange the cards exactly as shown in the picture and lift up any one card, the rest will follow.

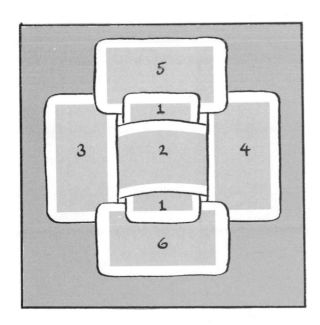

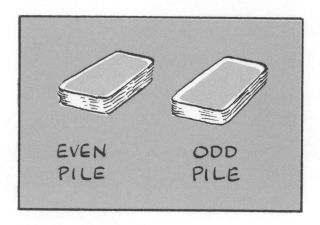

EVEN PILE   ODD PILE

20 Against the Odds

You show your friend a deck of cards divided into two piles. You say, "Take a card from either pile, look at it, and put it back into the middle of the *other* pile."

Now you pick up that other pile, go through the cards, and with a flourish you hand your bewildered buddy the card he or she just picked!

How did you know which card was selected?

Well, before you started, when you were alone, you put all the *even* cards—from two through queen—into one pile. You put all of the *odd* cards from ace through king together in another pile.

Now you'll have no trouble finding the chosen card because it will be the only misfit—either it will be the only even card with all the odd ones or vice versa.

As soon as you've handed your pal the chosen card, shuffle the two piles together and destroy the evidence!

Now they can even examine the cards!

THIS IS YOUR CARD, I BELIEVE!

21 Good Vibes

This trick will get "oh's" when you do it, and "oh, *no's!*" when your friends find out *how* you did it! Just make sure you have a trusty secret assistant.

HERE'S WHAT HAPPENS: You leave the room. Your assistant asks someone to pick a favorite number from one to ten. Then you are called back into the room. At this point you claim that you and your friend have such close communication that you can tell the number chosen from your friend's mental vibrations. You put your fingertips lightly on your friend's temples to pick up those mental vibrations.

HERE'S HOW: As you put your fingertips on the sides of your friend's head, your friend tightens his or her jaws. This makes the temples bulge out a little against your fingertips— you'll feel it right away. So if the chosen number is four, your friend must clamp his or her jaws shut four times. Pretty tricky and a real crowd stumper!

22 Secret Signal

Here's a trick to do at your next party or club meeting. It'll knock 'em out in school, too! And all you need is a secret assistant.

You go out of the room. The rest of the group picks some object in plain view of everyone. After you return, your assistant names various things around the room. When the right object is named, you instantly say, "That's the one you all picked!"

Now, you may ask, "How can the assistant let me know which is the right object?" But the truth is, the assistant can't! The secret of this very baffling mystery is that *you* are the one doing the signaling. Read on!

THE TRICK: You come back into the room and your friend starts naming or pointing to objects in different parts of the room. Four, five, or six objects are named. Then when you want the selected object to be named or pointed out, *you* do something to change your position—fold or unfold your arms, shift one foot, or put your hands behind you. Any natural and easy movement will do. As soon as your assistant sees you do this, the *next* object he or she names *must* be the selected one. As soon as it is called, you name it as the group's choice.

Just this once, let yourself be pressured into doing the same trick twice. Watch the fun and frustration grow. The secret of this particular while-I'm-out-of-the-room trick is that *everyone is watching and listening to your assistant*, waiting for a signal that will never come!

23 My Number One Trick

You can be the number one magician on your block! It's easy!

HERE'S HOW: Tell a group of friends—the more the merrier—"Pick a number from 1 to 5. Any number. Don't tell it to me. Double it. Now add 2. I'll wait. Now divide by 2. Remember your original number? Subtract that original number from what is left. Keep it a secret—don't tell anybody. Now, when I count three, everybody shout out the number that is left."

Everybody will shout out, "One." No matter what number they started with. Really!

You see? *Everybody* wants to be number one!

24 Thirty-four, Every Time

Here's a math magic trick that takes no math—it just uses numbers in a very funny way.

On a piece of paper write the numbers 1 through 16 in four rows of four across. Your square should look like the picture.

On another piece of paper, you—the magical whiz kid—write your secret final prediction. (Now, nobody knows it, but the number you are writing is 34.)

Next you say, "Pick a number, any number." Then *circle* whatever number your friend selects, and cross out all of the other numbers up and down in that line, and all of the numbers side to side in that line too (picture 1).

Next you say, "Pick *another* number— one that isn't circled or crossed out." You do the same thing this time (picture 2). Do it once again, so you have three circled numbers in all (picture 3). Now there's only one number left which is not circled or crossed out. Circle that one too (picture 4).

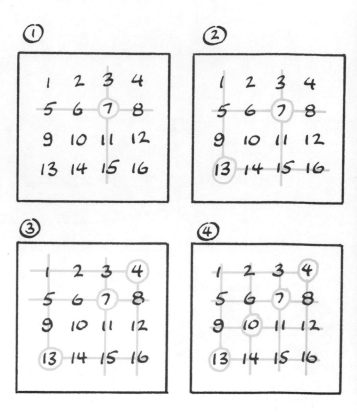

Add up all four of the *circled* numbers, and you'll find they *must* add up to 34! And that, of course, is the number you secretly wrote on that paper before you started!

I promise, no matter what numbers they call out and you circle, the final sum will always be 34!

25 Finger Math

Show your pals how you can multiply by nine on your fingers.

Hold your two hands in front of you, thumbs facing each other. If you want to figure out what 1 times 9 equals, bend down the pinky of your right hand. What's left is the answer: 1 times 9 equals 9—and there are 9 fingers sticking up.

For 2 times 9, bend down only your right ring finger. Again, what's left is the answer. On the left side of that bent ring finger is a 1, and on the other side 8 fingers are sticking up. So 2 times 9 equals 1 and 8—18. Figure out 3 times 9 by bending down only your right middle finger. To the left of that bent finger are 2 fingers sticking up, to the right, 7. So your answer is 27. That means 3 times 9 equals 27. Is that right? Yes, that's right!

I guess you can figure out the rest, but it's too amazing for me to stop now! Here's 4 times 9: Bend only the right pointer finger down, 3 fingers sticking up on one side, 6 on the other—36! (Which is what you get when you multiply 4 times 9, by cracky!)

26 Crayon Carbon Paper

This carbon paper can be used over and over.

HERE'S HOW: Crayon *heavily* all over a sheet of paper. Use lots of different colors on different parts of the paper. (Dark colors will work better than light ones.) Put this paper *face down* on top of a blank sheet of paper. Draw or write with a ball-point pen—press down hard—on the clean side of the crayoned sheet. (The clean side is, of course, on top facing you.) Your drawing or writing will transfer to the bottom sheet in a random, multicolored pattern. Add more color to the crayon "carbon" when your carbon pictures or words start becoming lighter.

27 Groaners

Some stunts make kids grin. Others make them groan. Those are groaners—dumb gags and sucker bets that have silly solutions. Like when you say to your pal, "I'll bet a quarter you can't take off that coat alone." And then as soon as your buddy starts to take off his or her coat, you take off *your* coat too—so your friend *can't* take off that coat alone.

GROANNN!

Or when you say to a friend, "I bet I can stay underwater for a full minute." When everyone says to prove it, you simply fill a glass with water and hold it over your head—for a full minute!

Your friends will groan when you tell them groaners, and then they will turn around and pull the same gag on the very next person they meet!

28 Cat's Cradle Escape

HERE'S WHAT YOU DO: Make a cat's cradle and have a friend put his arm up through the center. If you let go of the string with everything except your thumbs, you'll catch your friend's arm in a loop. Leaving your friend caught, you again make the cradle. Now your friend places his arm down through the center, and you pull. He'll be caught again, right? Wrong! This time he's set free!

HERE'S HOW YOU DO IT: Take a piece of string (at least 4 feet long) and knot the ends together. Stretch the loop between your two thumbs, palms facing each other. Then stick your pinky fingers up into the loop as well. The string will now be stretched across your palms and around the back of each thumb and pinky finger (picture 1). To make the cradle, bring the palms of the two hands together, slide the tip of the right middle finger under the loop around the left palm, separate the hands about 6 inches, then slide the left middle finger under the loop on the right palm. Pull back your hands until the cradle becomes tight (picture 2).

Now have your friend put his hand *up* through the center of the cradle (picture 3). Drop all your fingers except your thumbs out of the loops and pull. You will have caught your friend's wrist (picture 4). Don't let him free himself. Keep him in that loop, and make another cradle.

This time have him put his imprisoned hand *down* through the center (picture 5). Let all your fingers slip out of the string except your thumbs. When you pull this time, the string will seem to go right through your friend's wrist (picture 6)!

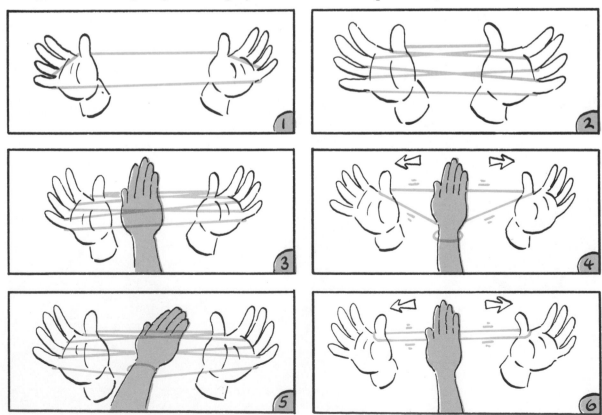

29 The Wandering Water Trick

Here's how you can make water vanish from one cup and reappear in another.

Before you do the trick, get three paper cups. Cut out the flat bottom of one paper cup. Then stack the three paper cups with the bottomless one (cup *B*) in the middle (see picture 1).

Now you're ready to perform.

Pour water from a pitcher into your top cup (cup *A*). Then lift cup *A* off the stack (see picture 2). Ask the audience which cup contains the water. When they say "cup *A*," you quickly agree, then ask them to keep their eyes on where the water goes.

Pick up cup *A* and pour the water from it into cup *B*—which doesn't have a bottom, remember? (See picture 3.) Next, lift up cup *B*. Make sure to hold it in your hand carefully so no one can see the bottom (see picture 4). Everybody will think that cup *B* has water in it, but because you

have secretly removed the bottom, the water has gone through into cup *C*.

Ask your audience where the water is now, and when they point to cup *B*, say, "Oh, no, you weren't watching."

Tilt cup *B*. Again do this carefully so your audience can't see the bottom. Then turn it upside down to show that it's empty. Now put the cup on the table (picture 5).

Pick up cup *C* and pour the water from it into cup *A*. The water will appear to have vanished from cup *B* and somehow "traveled" into cup *C* (picture 6).

Casually pile your cups back into one another, stacking them as before with the bottomless cup in the middle and the filled cup on the top.

Make sure to practice this trick in front of a mirror. Don't try to fool an audience until you can fool yourself!

30 Fishy Business

Make a fish using eight toothpicks (see picture *A*). The fish is facing in one direction. Moving only three toothpicks, can you end up with the same fish facing in the *opposite* direction?

HERE'S HOW: Remove the bottom fin (toothpick 8), the bottom of the tail (toothpick 7), and the bottom of the face (toothpick 4). They become the top fin, the top of the tail, and the top of the face in picture *B*.

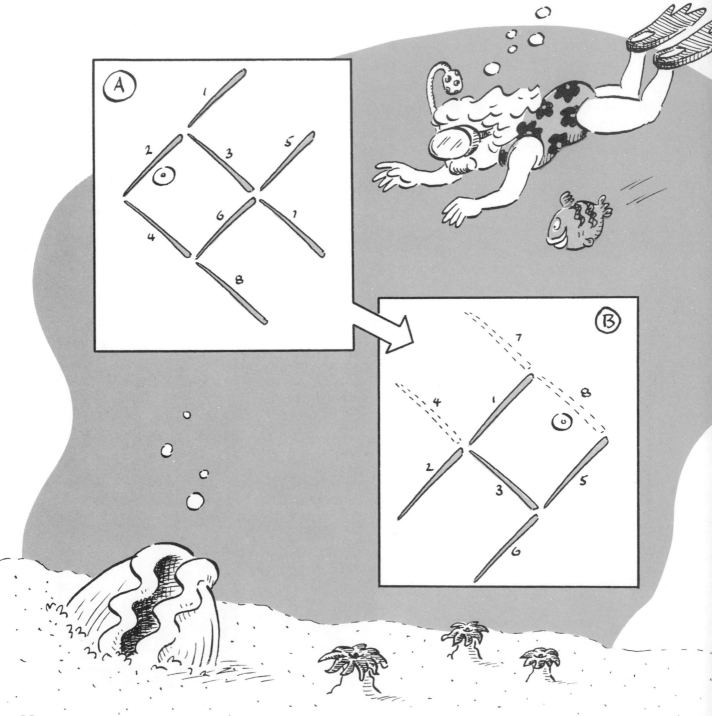

31 Tongue Twisters

Even if Peter Piper really did pick a peck of pickled peppers, who cares? Well, *somebody* must care, because people have been twisting their tongues around that silly phrase for years and years and years.

If you and your friends want to twist *your* tongues around some real jawbreakers, try these—three times fast!

- Double bubble gum bubbles double.
- A noise annoys an oyster.
- Greek grape leaves
- Good blood, bad blood
- I see icy icicles.
- Frank threw Fred three free throws.
- Rubber baby buggy bumpers
- Slick super-sleuth
- The sun shines on the shop signs.
- Preshrunk shirts
- A cup of proper coffee in a proper coffee cup

BATTY BUTTA BITTY BETTER...

You don't have to say all tongue twisters three times fast—some are hard enough just to say once! Like: "Betty bought a bit of butter. 'But,' she said, 'this butter's bitter. If I put it in my batter, it will make my batter bitter. But a bit of better butter will make my batter better.' So Betty bought a bit of better butter and it made her batter better."

Lots of tongue twisters are about animals: "Six sleek slippery seals"; "Sixty-six sick chicks"; "When a big black bug bit my big black bear, it made my big black bear bleed blood." Or the ever-popular "How much wood would a woodchuck chuck, if a woodchuck could chuck wood?"

32 Fortune Checkers

Here's a game of pure chance.

On tiny slips of paper (as in fortune cookies) write lots of different instructions. Here are some examples:

- Move one checker one square ahead.
- Move one checker one square back.
- Move two checkers two squares ahead.
- Move one checker three squares ahead.
- Don't do a thing. You've lost your turn! Sorry!
- Take one checker off the board now! Congratulations!
- All your checkers go back to their starting positions. Whoops!

Place these fortune slips into a bag or box and mix 'em up.

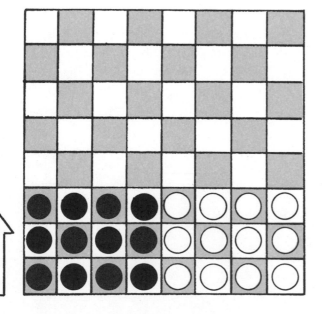

Now line up all of the checkers on a checkerboard as shown in the picture (black checkers on one side, red on the other).

You and a friend take turns pulling out a fortune slip from the bag. You must do exactly what it says on the paper (if you can't, you lose your turn). Put the fortune back in the bag after your turn.

In this game you play on every single square, and no jumping is allowed. What you want to do is move all your checkers forward to the end of the board and then off the board.

The first player to have all his or her checkers off the board is the winner.

33 Meet Your Match

Here's a game that you are almost sure to lose, but it's great fun to play anyway! Play alone or with friends.

Take the jokers out of a deck of cards. Shuffle and put the pack face down on the table. Then call out the names of the cards in their regular sequence—"Ace, two, three," right up through "king." As you say each card's name, you turn over the top card of the deck. The point of the game is to be wrong every single time. You score a point for every "wrong" call.

The funny thing is that it's almost impossible to get through the whole deck without coming up with a match. If you're lucky enough to get from ace all the way through king once without a match, start again with ace.

If you play with a friend, you each get to go through the cards until you get caught with a match. Then it's the next person's turn. Each player gets five turns. The winner is the one with the most points.

34 Water, Water Everywhere

Are you game for a game? All you and your friends need is a fistful of pennies.

Go into the kitchen and fill a paper cup or coffee mug full of water, right to the brim. Leave the cup in the sink.

Now lean over the sink and take turns gently slipping the pennies into the cup one at a time. *The one who makes the water overflow is the loser.*

Or if that game sounds all wet, try this one: Fill a paper cup or coffee mug full of water, cover it with a paper napkin, and fasten the napkin in place with a rubber band. Put a penny on the napkin.

Now you and your friends take turns poking holes in the napkin with the point of a pencil. The one who pokes the hole that causes the coin to drop into the water is the loser.

IT'S **GOT** TO DROP THIS TIME!

RUBBER BAND

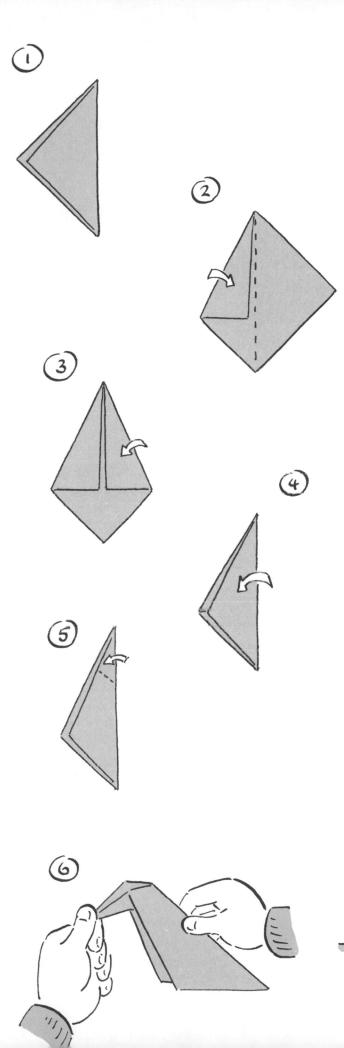

35 The Hungry Crow

Would you like a pet that loves to eat? Here's how you can make one.

Take a square of paper. Fold it in half so that the top corner meets the bottom corner (picture 1). Open up the paper and fold one edge over so that it meets the center fold (picture 2). Fold the other edge over so that it too meets the center fold. Now you have a kite shape (picture 3).

Fold the kite shape in half along the center crease (picture 4). At an angle, crease the top point back and forth, and then straighten the point (picture 5). With one hand, pinch the center fold directly below this slanting crease. Put the thumb of your other hand on top of the center crease, grasping the point between these two fingers. Pull down until the center crease forms a valley between your two hands (picture 6). With your left hand, sharpen all these new creases.

Set your crow down so that it is balancing on its nose and two center points. Tap its tail gently and it will peck at tiny crumpled balls of paper (picture 7).

36 The Floating Pencil

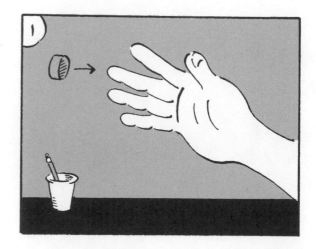

Do you have double-faced tape? If not, *before* you do this trick, make a ring of tape with the sticky side on the outside (see picture 1). Secretly slip this ring onto the tip of your right middle finger. Now place a pencil so that it's sticking up out of a cup, and you're ready to fool 'em!

To do The Floating Pencil trick, clasp your hands together with fingers interlaced, but with the right middle finger secretly hidden in your palm (picture 2).

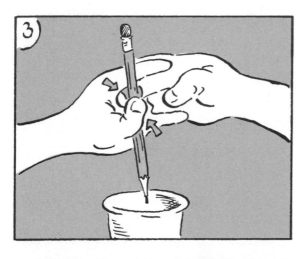

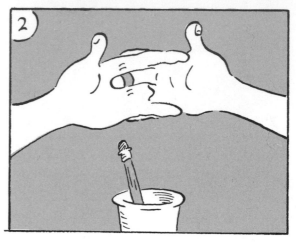

Bend that hidden finger behind your other fingers. Slide your hands down in front of the pencil and grab the pencil so it's pressed between the sticky tip of your middle finger and your two thumbs.

Lift your thumbs carefully—as though you're doing something wonderful—and the pencil will look like it's floating (picture 3). Now move your finger so that the pencil waves mysteriously in the air (picture 4). Make sure your thumbs are sticking straight up, so no one thinks they're holding the pencil. When you put the pencil back down into the cup, pinch it between the pointer finger and the thumb of your *other* hand and pull it away from your taped finger.

37 Card Castle

Ever try building a card castle? It's really frustrating—hard to get started because the cards slip, and annoying because you never know when "just one more" is going to be too many!

However, you *can* build a card castle that won't be gone with the wind!

As soon as you lose one card out of the 52 cards in a deck, that deck is useless for most card games. But you now have a set of 51—or 50 or 49 or whatever's left— "building blocks" for constructing card castles.

HERE'S HOW: First of all, start on a rug, rather than on a hard floor. Then on one card, cut the pattern shown in the picture. Snip in along all the little black lines. Lay this pattern on each card in your deck. Trace those little lines onto the card and then make the slits.

By fitting a slit on one card into a slit on another, you can start building. Hold two cards parallel to each other. Place a third card so that it goes across the top of the first two. If you insert the slits of the third card into the slits of the other two, the three cards should stand on their own.

Carefully add lots more cards, and your card castle is on its way up!

38 Me, Myself, and I

The next time you and a group of friends are sitting around with nothing to do, say to your friends, "I've been studying new techniques for self-control and I can do amazing things to myself. I can make myself all wrinkled. I can rip myself in half. I can even throw myself on the floor and step all over myself."

Your pals will probably giggle and tell you that what you said is weird—and then you can prove that everything you said is true.

HERE'S HOW: Show your friends a piece of paper on which the word "myself" is written. Then crinkle it up in your hand—now it's all wrinkled. Rip it in half. Then throw the pieces on the floor and jump all over them. The best way to pull off this silly stunt is to write the word "myself" on a slip of paper ahead of time, fold the paper up, and keep it out of sight, in the palm of your hand, till you're ready.

36

39 The "Giant" Penny

Say to a friend, "Do you have a penny? Look at it. Now look at the tabletop in this picture. It looks bigger than a penny, doesn't it? But I'll bet there's no way that you can put your penny down on the table in this picture without the penny touching two of the edges of the tabletop." There's no trick to this—it simply can't be done. The size of the tabletop is an optical illusion.

40 From A to Z

Can you make a sentence that uses all the letters in the alphabet? I'm sure lots of sentences can be put together, but the one I like best is easy to remember: "The quick brown fox jumps over the lazy dog." (Go ahead. Check it out. They're all there!)

41 The Reversible Word

What four-letter word reads the same forward, backward, and upside down?

GIVE UP? THE FOUR-LETTER WORD IS "NOON."

42 Topsy-turvy Year

What year in this century looks exactly the same *upside down*?

THE ANSWER IS 1961. GO AHEAD. TURN IT UPSIDE DOWN.

43 Alphariddles

What word starts with an *E* and usually contains only one letter?

"ENVELOPE." IT STARTS WITH AN *E* AND IT USUALLY CONTAINS ONLY ONE LETTER.

What occurs once in a minute, twice in a moment, and never in a thousand years?

THE LETTER *M*.

44 Down the Chute

This coin trick is great because you don't have to prepare anything ahead of time. And when they see it, your dumbfounded friends will agree that keeping track of money isn't easy!

HERE'S WHAT YOUR FRIENDS SEE: You're sitting at a table. You wrap a coin in a square of paper, and then tear up the paper to show that the coin has vanished.

HERE'S HOW: Start with a piece of paper about 4 inches square. Place the coin in the center of the paper (picture 1). *Hold the paper in your hands*—don't put it on the table. Fold up the bottom third to cover the coin (picture 2), and fold down the top third over that. Turn the paper a quarter-turn and as you fold the top down let the coin slide out of the bottom opening into your hand and hide it in your lap (see picture 3). Now fold up the bottom. Hold up the packet, say your magic words, and then tear the packet in half to show that the coin has disappeared.

Easy come, easy go!

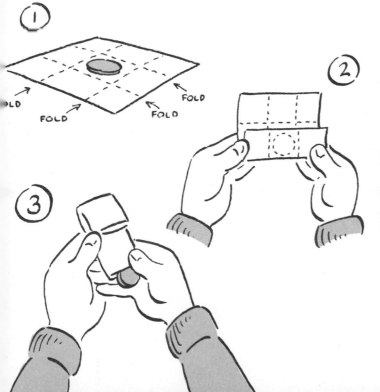

45 Money Talks

Here's a trick in which a dollar bill will say "hello" to you!

Borrow five one-dollar bills and toss them on a table. A friend picks one and writes its serial number on a piece of paper. (The picture shows you where the serial number is on a bill.) Then that friend crumples the other bills into wads. *You wad up the bill that was chosen* and mix it with the rest. Hold one crumpled-up bill after another up to your ear. Finally, you discover which one was picked, because it said "hello" to you. Open the bill, check the serial number, and—wonder of wonders—you've picked the right bill.

SERIAL NUMBER

HIDDEN NICKEL

HERE'S HOW: Have a nickel hidden in your lap. As your pal is writing the number, put the nickel in your hand. Take the bill, read the number back to your friend, and crumple it into a ball. As you wad the bill up, *wrap it around the nickel*. Put it on the table with the other wadded-up money. Turn your head away and mix the bills all around.

One by one, hold the bills to your ear so you can hear the special bill talk. What you're really doing is squeezing each one. When you feel the lump of the nickel, unwrap that bill, hiding the nickel in your hand. Give the bill to your friend who has the paper with the serial number. Your pal will be amazed that you've picked the right one, and as you bow be sure to say "thank you" to the dollar bill that said "hello" to you.

HELLO!

46 The First-Name Trick

How would you like to show all your friends that you can read words written on a piece of paper held in somebody else's hand?

You would? Read on!

Sit at a table or a desk and ask your friends to call out the first names of a number of well-known people or classmates. As each name is called, write it on a scrap of paper, fold the paper up, and drop it into a paper bag.

Ask somebody to reach into the bag and take out just one of those scraps of paper. Then you hold the bag to your forehead and concentrate very hard.

At long last you relax and tell everybody the name that is written on the piece of paper held by the other person.

Your friend unfolds the paper and—lo and behold!—you are absolutely correct!

How did you do it? Easy!

On every single scrap of paper you write only the *first* name that is called. After all, nobody can see what you're scribbling. Since the same name is written on all the papers, there's no way that you can make a mistake!

47 Get the Point

Scorekeeping is an important part of any game, but don't trust it to memory because you might find that every player "remembers" a different score at the end of the game.

Since paper and pencil are rarely handy when you need 'em, I've found a few fast and funny ways to keep a record of "who-gets-how-many-points."

1. If you have a lot of string, give a long piece to each player. When a point is won, the player makes a knot in the string. At the end of the game, the one with the greatest number of knots is the winner.

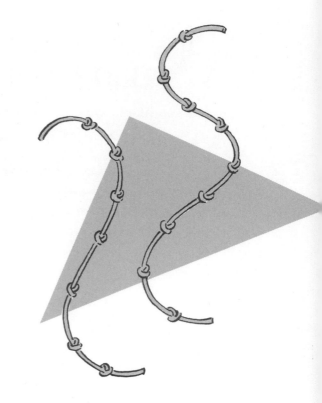

2. Roll bits of tissue into little balls and give, say, ten to each player. Then whenever one person wins a point, the other player has to give him or her a tissue ball. The game is over when one player has won all of the opponents' little balls. (Pennies, pebbles, shells, or beans can be substituted for the paper balls.)

3. If you have paper cups in the house, and if you give each player a cup, you can keep score on the rim of it. For each point gained, the player tears a tiny slit along the top rim of the cup.

4. Before you start a game, each player gets a tablespoon and a full glass of a favorite drink. Then every time a point is scored, that player removes and drinks one tablespoonful from his or her glass. The first player to empty a glass wins.

48 For Girls Only

Place a chair sideways near a wall, but not quite touching it. A man or grown boy leans over until his head rests against the wall, with his back straight and parallel to the floor, and with his feet spaced the same width as the chair.

Now he has to *lift the chair and then stand up with it.* He utterly fails! However, every girl or woman in the room does it with ease!

HERE'S HOW: The only preparation for this startling challenge is to be born a female! Females are able to lift the chair and stand up because their hips are placed differently and give a counterbalance to the rest of the body in that position.

To be specific, you should place an armless kitchen or dining room chair sideways to the wall and about an inch away from it. Have a boy or man place his feet about an inch away from the chair legs and spaced exactly the same distance apart (see picture). Tell him to grip the seat of the chair as shown and to lean over until his back is level and his head is resting against the wall. Now challenge him to lift the chair straight up (which is fairly easy) and then to lift *himself* to a standing position while still holding the chair (which is impossible!).

49 **Your Mighty Fingertips**

Touch the tips of your two pointer fingers together in front of you, with your elbows out. Now press your fingers together hard. Your friend will find that—holding your wrists and pulling without jerking—it's almost impossible to pull those fingertips apart.

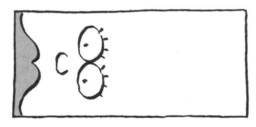

50 **Big Mouth**

You will need:

> A calling (business) card or any small, stiff, rectangular piece of paper
> A pencil, crayon, or pen

HERE'S HOW: Draw two eyes and a nose near one end of the card (picture 1). Bend but do not fold the rectangle in half with your left thumb on top, middle finger on the bottom, and your pointer finger sandwiched between the two layers (picture 2). Place your right thumb and middle finger on opposite sides at the bend of the paper. Press the knuckle of your right pointer finger against this bend until you create a slight dent.

Now lift this right pointer finger and take away your left hand (picture 3). Simply press your right thumb and middle finger together slightly. Big Mouth will talk and talk and talk!

51 A Rough Trick

You tear a piece of paper into nine squares. Have eight people write any even number on a square. Then ask a person to write an odd number on the ninth square of paper. The squares are turned over so the numbers don't show and then shifted about to mix them up well. You just take one look and, even though you can't see the numbers, you point to the only square with the odd number!

HERE'S HOW: Fold a big piece of paper in thirds. Tear the paper along these folds. You have three strips now. Tear the tall strips into thirds. You now have nine pieces of paper, all about the same size. Scatter them on the table. One by one, hand out eight of the squares of paper to friends and ask them to write an even number on their square. When you hand out the squares, make sure *not* to hand out the one square of paper with four rough (torn) edges. Save that square until the very end. Give it to the ninth person and ask him or her to write down an odd number on it.

Ask that all the papers be turned over (so the numbers are hidden) and mixed up.

And you will know right away which square contains the odd number! It's the only one with four rough edges.

THIS ONE HAS THE ODD NUMBER!

52 Snap Gun

Bang! That's the sound this little snap gun will make if you fold it right.

Make your snap gun out of a large square sheet of newspaper.

Fold the square corner to corner so that it becomes a triangle (picture 1). Open it up. Now fold the square corner to corner so that the *other* two corners meet to make a triangle. Once again, open it up (picture 2). Then fold your square in half. This time, don't open it up (picture 3). Push in the two side triangles (the shaded parts in picture 3). Make the folds nice and sharp (picture 4).

Now slip your pointer finger in between two of the points on one side, hold the outer flaps (picture 5), and snap your wrist down hard! The fold on the other side of your snap gun will pop open with a loud *crack!*

53 Add-a-Word

Playing Add-a-Word is like eating peanuts—once you start, you get hooked and don't want to stop. Play Add-a-Word alone or with any number of friends.

HERE'S HOW: For each player, write out the entire alphabet and under each letter write a number—1 through 26, in order. Now give each player a piece of paper. The challenge is to write down 12 words of three letters each. Each letter is worth a certain number of points, so each word has a total value. For example, "wow" (23 plus 15 plus 23) is worth 61 points; "zoo" (26 plus 15 plus 15) is worth only 56. If you are playing this game with friends, the player with the highest 12-word total wins the game.

A	B	C	D	E	F	G	H	I	J	K	L	M
1	2	3	4	5	6	7	8	9	10	11	12	13

N	O	P	Q	R	S	T	U	V	W	X	Y	Z
14	15	16	17	18	19	20	21	22	23	24	25	26

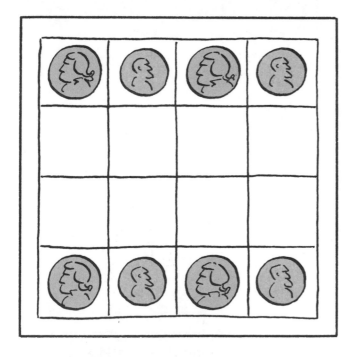

54 Four in a Row

This game is for two players. You divide a piece of paper into 16 squares, four rows of four squares each. Get four nickels and four pennies and arrange them on the playing board as shown: nickel, penny, nickel, penny. One player moves pennies and the other moves nickels.

The players take turns moving one coin in any direction, but only one square at a time. There is no "jumping" over any coins, and two coins can't be on the same square.

The winner is the first player who gets all four coins in a straight line. They can go up and down, side to side, or on the diagonal. They just have to be in one straight line and on squares that are next to one another.

55 Join-a-Coin

To play this game, first you have to make your own Join-a-Coin game board. It's easy. Just draw a very large square. Inside the square draw four lines up and down and four lines side to side—all evenly spaced. You now have 25 boxes inside your big square, and you're ready to play Join-a-Coin!

Gather a pile of pennies for yourself and a pile of nickels for your friend. First you get to put one of your coins in a box, then the other player puts one of his or her coins in another box. You take turns putting down coins, one at a time, until one of the players has five coins in a row. It doesn't matter whether the row is vertical (up and down), horizontal (across), or on the diagonal—if you've joined five of your coins in a row, you're the champ!

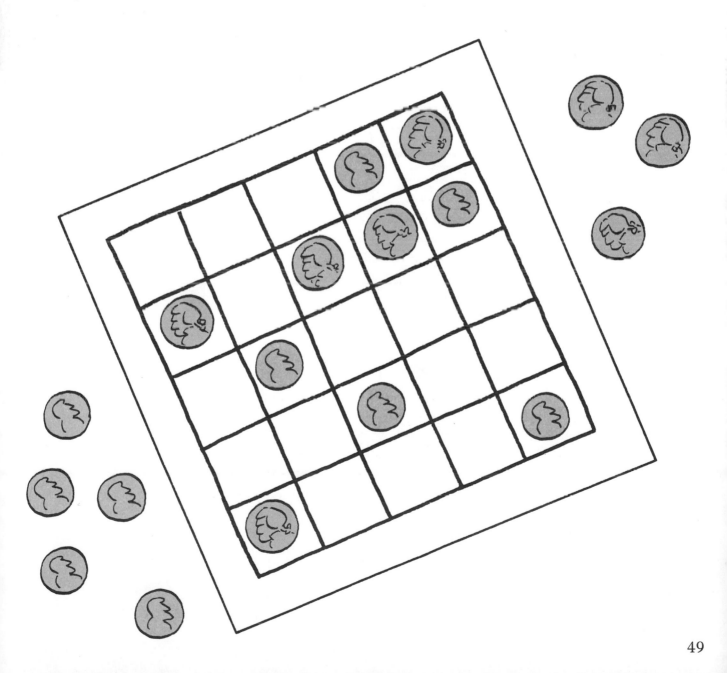

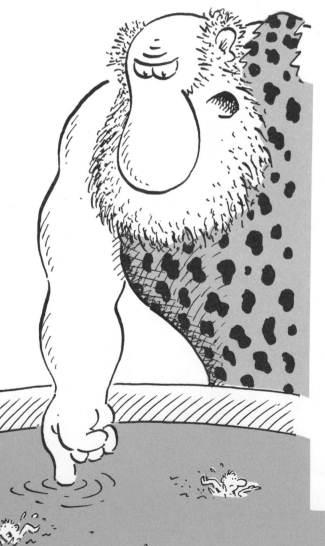

OUT OF MY BOWL, SMALL FRY!

56 Scared Pepper

Here's a story and an experiment all wrapped up in one.

FIRST, THE EXPERIMENT: If you fill a bowl with water and sprinkle black pepper all over the water, the pepper will stay on top, covering the entire surface of the water. But if you soap up your finger and stick it into the center of the water, the pepper will "run away" from your finger.

NOW FOR THE STORY: "A giant was bothered by tiny little people who constantly went swimming in his bowl." As you say this, sprinkle on the pepper. "He thought and thought, but couldn't figure out what to do. To make matters worse, the people were the dirtiest things he'd ever seen. They never used soap, and he certainly didn't want them floating in the center of *his* bowl! So one day he soaped up his giant finger and stuck it right into the middle of the bowl." Now stick your soaped-up finger into the center of the bowl. "The giant was very happy to see that all the people scurried away as fast as they could."

Why does the pepper run away from the soaped finger? The oil from the soap dissolves and literally pushes the pepper away as it spreads over the surface of the water.

57 Catch-a-Buck

Here's an almost impossible stunt to do with a dollar bill that might even have amused George Washington.

Crease a dollar bill in half the long way. Then grasp it at the top between your thumb and index finger.

Now ask your friend to place one hand behind his or her back and to hold the other hand so that the palm is open and next to the bill, but not touching it.

You drop the bill. Your friend tries to catch it but can't because in the split second it takes to react, the bill will have already slipped past your pal's fingers.

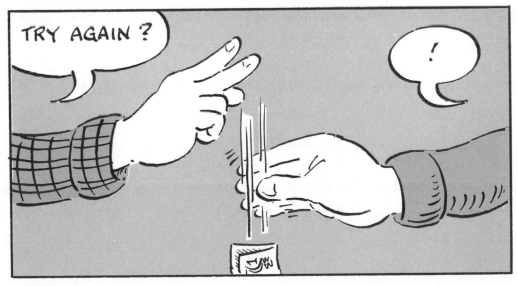

58 So Near and Yet So Far

Ask a friend to put one hand on his or her hip and stand with heels against the wall and knees straight. Drop a dollar bill (or a ten-dollar bill if you wish—you're safe!) right in front of the person. Now say, "If you can pick up that bill without bending your knees—just bend over slowly, pick it up, and stand up again—you can keep it."

Don't sweat it—the money is yours!

59 Flip-flop

Take a one-dollar bill and a five-dollar bill. Place the one-dollar bill on top of the five-dollar bill. Tell your friends, "I know you won't believe this, but I can make these bills switch places."

HERE'S HOW: Lay the five-dollar bill on the table so one of the short sides is facing you and the other is facing your audience. Now cover the five-dollar bill with the one-dollar bill so that the top bill extends a little past the lower bill in the direction of the audience. Starting at the lower left corner, roll both bills onto a pencil. Keep rolling until one little flap flips free of the roll. It will be the flap of the five-dollar bill. Put your finger on it, then *unroll* the pencil *toward you*. Magically, the bills will have reversed themselves, and the five-dollar bill, which started out on the bottom, is now on top!

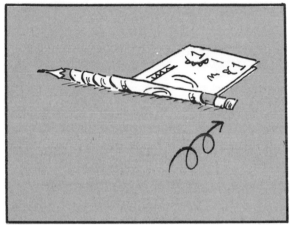

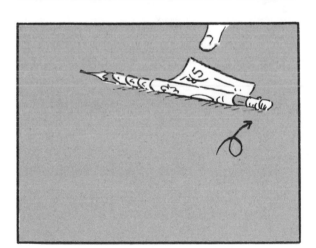

60 Line 'Em Ups

If you know stunts that can be done with coins, you're always ready for action. You can reach into your pocket anytime, anywhere, and pull out your props.

Place 12 coins in a square so that there are four coins in each row as shown. Now, can you move these coins into another figure that has five in each row?

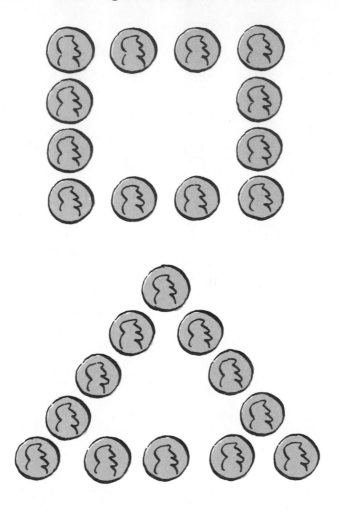

That was easy.

Now let's start with just six coins this time. To make two rows of three coins each is simple. But can you make two rows of four coins each? Two ways are possible, as you can see!

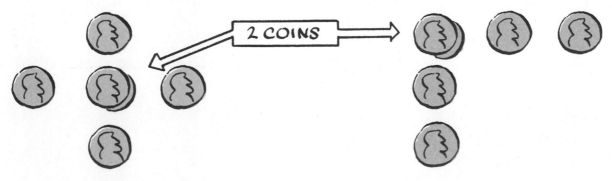

61 All Heads, All Tails

Lay out nine pennies, alternating heads and tails, in three rows of three pennies each. The first row starts with a heads-up penny, then one that is tails up, and the last, heads up. The next row starts with a tails-up coin, and the last row begins with a heads-up coin. Make sure the three rows of coins are close together.

HERE'S THE CHALLENGE: Can you make the first and the third horizontal (across) rows become *all heads*? If you do so, the middle row will become all tails.

HERE'S THE CATCH: *You must do this by touching only one coin!*

HERE'S HOW: Place your finger on the tails-up penny at the top of the second vertical (up and down) row. Move it up and swing it around all the rest of the pennies and down to the bottom of that same vertical row. Turn it over so that it is heads up. Now (with that penny) push up against the other two pennies in that row, until they've all pushed up one row.

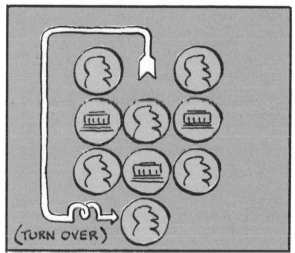

(TURN OVER)

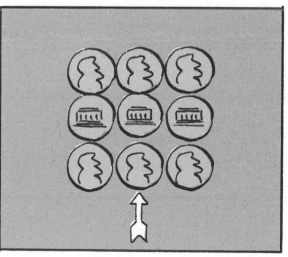

SEE, I'M ONLY TOUCHING ONE COIN!

62 Tricks with Sticks

When you try these stunts on your friends, you can use toothpicks, cotton swabs, or even pencils, if you have enough. First take three sticks, make a triangle, and say, "A triangle has three sides and uses three sticks (picture 1). Can you make *two* triangles using only five sticks, without bending or breaking them?" (And when your pals give up, you add the two sticks below the triangle so that the bottom line of the first triangle becomes the top line of the second one. It will look like this (picture 2).

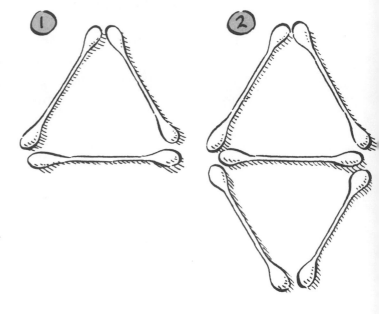

Here's another stick stunt. Count out five sticks and put them into your friend's hand. Then count out four more sticks and say, "How many is that, all together?" Your friend will say "nine," right?

Then you say, "Wrong! I will show you how five and four can make ten." When the protesting stops, you go to work!

Lay out four sticks in a row, a couple of inches apart from one another. Count out, "One, two, three, four."

Then take the other five sticks and, counting "One, two, three, four, five" as you lay them down, add the five sticks to the four so that they do indeed write TEN!

That wasn't really such a stick-y problem, was it?

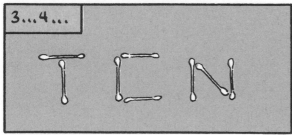

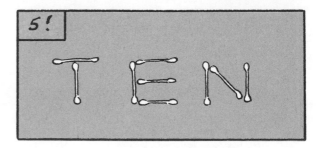

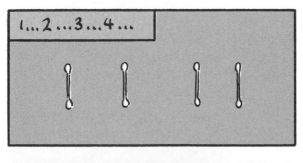

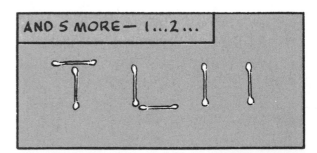

63 Funny Bunny

Here's a rabbit you can pull out of your pocket anytime.

You will need:

    An old handkerchief
    A rubber band

HERE'S HOW: Hold the handkerchief by the two top corners (picture 1). Place both corners together and hold the handkerchief with the two corners sticking above your fist (picture 2). These are the bunny ears. Now wind the bottom end of the handkerchief around your fingers that are holding the two ends (picture 3). Make a knot in the very same spot where you were holding the handkerchief.

The knot forms the bunny's face. (Add on features with markers.) Shove your pointer finger deep into the knot (behind the face) and drape the rest of the handkerchief around your hand. Loop a rubber band around your thumb, pull it in back of the puppet, and hook it on your middle finger. Presto! You've got yourself a bunny!

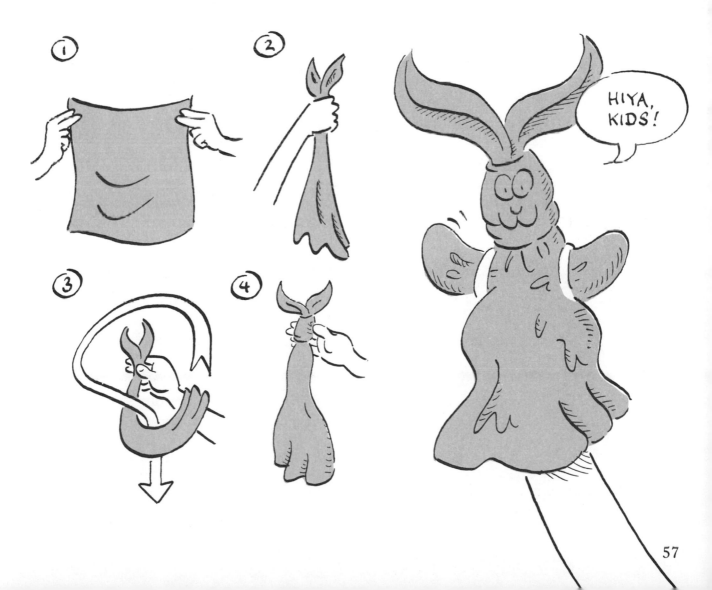

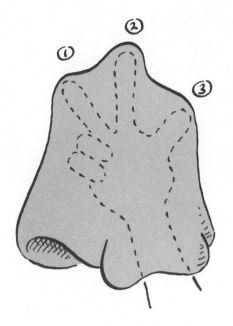

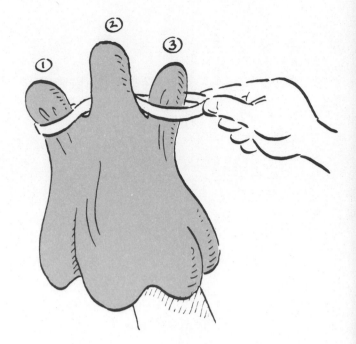

64 Instant Puppet Body

This puppet body will support a ball head, or a cup head, a hollowed egg, or any other object with a hole in the bottom.

You will need:

> A large handkerchief
> A rubber band

HERE'S HOW: Hold your hand with the last two fingers folded onto the palm and the other three fingers straight out. Now drape a handkerchief evenly over the extended fingers. Hook a rubber band over the handkerchief around your middle finger (number 1) and pull it around the *back* of your pointer finger (2); then hook it over your thumb (3).

The puppet head is placed over your pointer finger (2). The thumb and middle fingers (1 and 3) become your new puppet's hands—and there it is, right at your fingertips, ready to do your bidding.

65 The Rising Card

Some magic tricks work with strings, others with mirrors or magnets or trap doors.

This is a trick that you can make work using nothing but your bare hands!

HERE'S WHAT HAPPENS: You ask a friend to pick a card and put it on top of the deck. Then you will slip the deck back into its original package. Lo and behold! Wonder of wonders! Will miracles never cease? The selected card will rise up into view!

How can you make such a thing happen with your bare hands?

Simple! Before you perform this trick, cut a rectangle out of the back of the package. This opening must be big enough so that when the deck is put back into the pack, your thumb can push up on the card nearest to it—the top card of the deck! Just be sure to hold the card box carefully so that your audience never sees the hole.

HOW COME **I** CAN'T KNOCK **YOUR** FIST OFF?

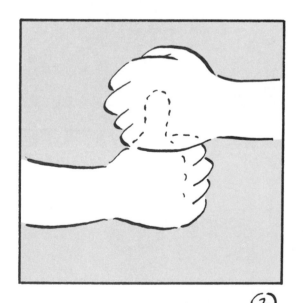

66 Strong Finger, Weak Fists

Say to a friend, "Make two fists. Put one fist on top of the other." When your friend has done that, say, "I'll bet I can knock your fists apart with one finger" (picture 1). Then with your pointer finger gently hit your friend's top fist right off the bottom one!

Now you say, "I'll betcha you can't do that to me." You put one fist on top of the other, and your pal cannot knock them apart!

HERE'S THE SECRET: When you put one fist on top of the other, secretly stick the thumb of your bottom hand up into the top fist and grip it tightly for support (picture 2). (Don't let anyone see you do this!) Strike as they will, your friends won't be able to separate your fists.

67 Envelope Bird

This envelope bird puppet is worth writing home about.

You will need:

An envelope
A crayon

HERE'S HOW: Place your hand into an envelope. Pick one that is the right size, so you can tuck your fingers into the corners. At the arrow, press in with the fingers of your other hand. Now as you open and close your hand inside the envelope, your bird will open and close its beak. Complete your bird by coloring in an eye. Your talking envelope bird is sure to win the stamp of approval!

To get your puppet to cling to your hand, lick the sticky stuff on the flap of the envelope, and you and your new bird friend will be inseparable.

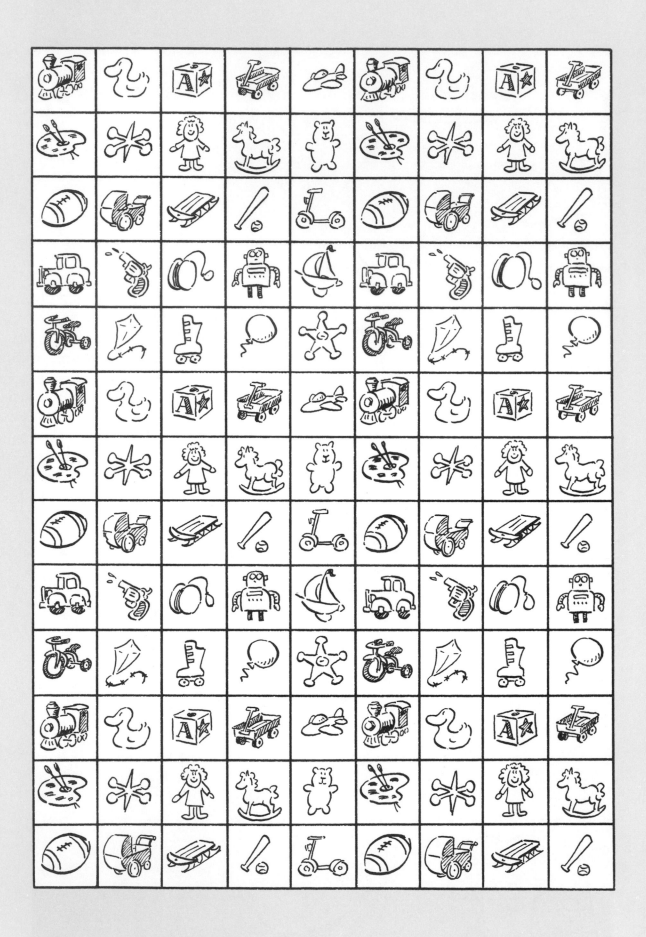

68 Hidden Toys

WHAT HAPPENS: You show your friends a piece of paper filled with pictures of lots and lots of different toys (see the picture on the opposite page). You turn your back so that you can't see the picture and you say, "Put a dime on any one of the squares. It will completely hide the toy in that square." Then when you turn around, you can immediately tell them which toy is hidden!

HERE'S HOW: All you have to do is count five squares *away* from the dime—either horizontally (across) or vertically (up and down)—and you will find the same toy as the one hidden under the dime. When you count, don't start *on* the dime, but start your counting in the square *next to* the dime.

69 Magic Number Box

Copy the box below, which is full of numbers, onto a 3- by 5-inch card or piece of paper and take it to school with you. You'll be able to do one of the best number tricks I've ever seen.

Say to a friend, "Pick any number on this piece of paper. Tell me which vertical (up and down) row you see it in. If you see it in *more* than one row, tell me which ones. And I will tell you the number you picked."

HERE'S HOW: When your friend tells you which rows the number is in, *take the top number in each of those rows* and add them together. Suppose your pal picked 5; 5 is found in the first and third rows. The number at the top of the first row is 1, and the number at the top of the third row is 4. When you add 1 and 4 you get 5, which is the number your friend thought of.

PICK ANY NUMBER ON THIS PIECE OF PAPER!

1	2	4	8
3	3	5	9
5	6	6	10
7	7	7	11
9	10	12	12
11	11	13	13
13	14	14	14

70 The Crowded Bus

See how closely your friends pay attention when you tell this story:

"You're driving a bus, and 32 people get on. Then 14 people get off. Then 130 people get on. Next 9 people get off. Then 2 people get on and 120 people get off. At the next stop 19 people get on. Finally, 36 people get off."

The question is this: What color are the bus driver's eyes?

ANSWER: The bus driver's eyes are whatever color *your* friend's eyes are. After all, the first thing you said was "You're driving a bus . . . !"

71 Super Speller

Say to someone who has a pretty long name, "I bet I can spell your name backward in the same length of time it takes me to do it forward." Sounds tough? It isn't. First spell the friend's name. Then just turn yourself around, so you're standing backward, and spell the name again!

72 Month Magic

"Thirty days hath September, April, June, and November"—or is it December? Frankly, I never learned that little rhyme because I knew that if I wanted to know whether a month had 30 or 31 days, I always had that information very handy. Not at my fingertips, but on my knuckles.

You do too. Hold your left hand palm down. Make a fist with your left hand. See how the knuckles are high points, like mountains? And between each of the four knuckles is a low point—a valley.

With the pointer finger of your right hand, touch your first knuckle and call it January. It's a high point (a mountain), so you know that January has the "high" number of days—31.

Now point to the valley next to that January mountain. Call the valley February. It's lower, so you know that it has a lower number of days. (In the weird case of February, that's either 28 or 29.)

Next to February is March—a mountain. Thirty-one days again. Then point to the valley next to March. That's April, and like all low months except February, April has only 30 days.

And so it goes. As you can see, July lands on a mountain (31 days). From July you switch to the first knuckle of your right hand. That first knuckle, or mountain, is for August (31 days), followed by September, down in the valley, with 30. (Remember "Thirty days hath September"?) And so it goes, on through December.

When you show this to your friends, I'll bet no one will ever fight with you about whether or not it works—because you'll be standing in front of them with your hand already in a fist!

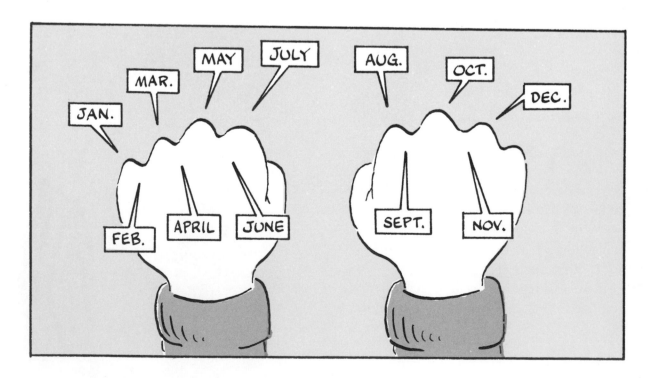

73 Lickety-split

Your friends'll think you're stuck on this card trick—until they discover that it's just a joke!

Ask your pal to pick a card—yes, yes, *any* card—and put it back *on top* of the deck. Now say, "I know what card you chose, and I'm going to send a mental picture of your card to some other person in the room."

Stand with your back to the buddy who picked the card—so that you are facing someone else. Press the deck to your forehead and say, "I'm concentrating very hard on sending the name of this card." Then the person you're facing will be able to name the card that was picked, lickety-split!

And I do mean LICKety-split!

HERE'S HOW: The selected card was put on top of the deck. As you turn around, secretly lick your finger and moisten your forehead. When you press the deck against your forehead, the top card will stick to your forehead, face outward. For a moment, take the rest of the deck away from your forehead, and the person you are facing will be able to read the selected card! Then grab the card before it falls off your forehead and spoils this super stumper!

You'll need to practice this trick before you try it on an audience—the tricky part is to take the deck away without removing the top card from your forehead.

74 The Blow-hard Card

Since most magicians show you tricks that can be done with playing cards, I thought you'd like to learn a trick that you *can't* do with a playing card.

Take a card from an old incomplete deck. (Please, don't be a joker and use a card from one of your folks' good decks or they'll never forgive me!)

Bend the card down about ¾ of an inch from each end. Then stand the card on a tabletop.

Now, here's the trick that can't be done. Challenge your friends to blow as hard as they wish, but no matter how much they blow, the card will remain standing on its own two little legs! It can't be blown over.

POSSIBLE 1ST PERSON'S MOVE

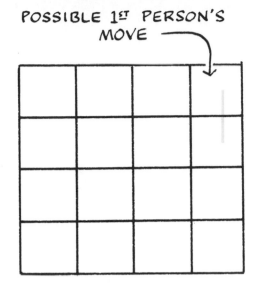

POSSIBLE 2ND PERSON'S MOVE

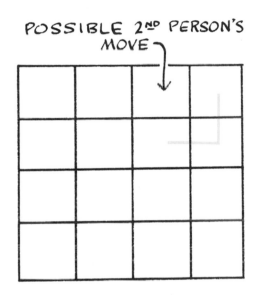

75 Line-a-Round

With this game, you can fill those pockets of time when you're waiting in a doctor's office, or lying on the beach, or just looking for something fun to do.

Draw a big square. Inside the square, draw three lines down and three lines across so you've got 16 little boxes inside the big square. The first player starts by making a line through a side of one of the little boxes. It doesn't matter which one. The other person then begins at either end of the first player's line, and crosses through another side of the *same* box. (However, if the first player's line goes through the *outside* of the big square, the second player can make the line continue on the outside of the square and come into another box.) *No side of any box may be crossed more than once.*

The object of this game is to bring the two ends of the continuous line into one box, which will then have *all four sides crossed once.* At this point, the player who has the next move loses because he has nowhere to go, since you are not allowed to cross any side twice.

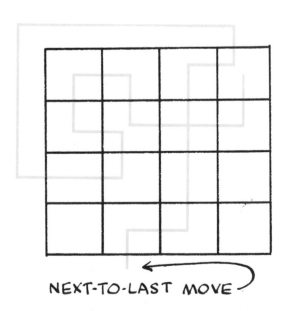

NEXT-TO-LAST MOVE

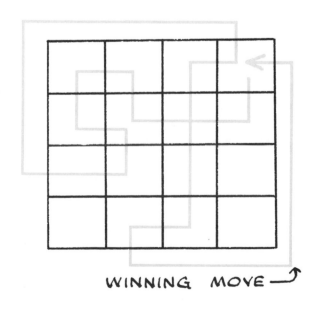

WINNING MOVE

76 Sock-er

Here's a game for a rainy, stuck-in-the-house day.

Dig into your family's clothes closet and pull out a half-dozen pairs of shoes—some of Dad's, Mom's, and your own. Line up the shoes against the wall in three rows—the biggest nearest the wall, middle-sized shoes in the middle, and then the smallest shoes in the very first row, closest to you and the other players.

Find three small pairs of socks. Roll each pair tightly into a ball. Put a rubber band around each sock ball.

One at a time, toss the sock balls into the shoes.

The biggest shoes are the easiest targets, so they are worth the fewest points. The smallest shoes are the toughest targets, so they get the greatest number of points.

77   **Ice Magic**

Can you float an ice cube in a glass of water for a minute without the ice cube ever touching the sides of the glass?

HERE'S HOW: First put the cube into the empty glass. Then slowly fill the glass with water until it overflows. The curved surface on the top of the water will keep the ice away from the glass.

78 The Missing Arrow

Adding only two straight lines, can you make a third arrow just like the two in the picture?

The dotted lines show you how!

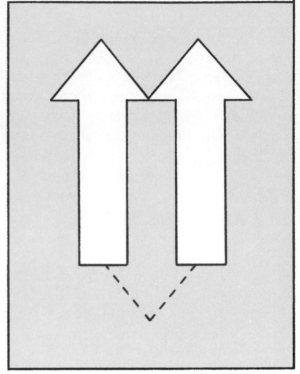

79 Rubber Face

People will groan when you do this stunt, but that's only because they didn't think of it first.

You boast, "I betcha I can stick out my tongue and touch my ear," and when the others are all done twisting their faces into funny positions as they try to stretch their tongues over to their ears, you simply do what you said you were going to do in the first place: stick out your tongue and then, with your hand, *touch your ear!*

80 The Weak Spot

Have a pal stand up. Say, "I'm going to put my finger on a certain spot on your face and I promise that you will not be able to move forward. The only rule is this—you may not move your feet."

And you can make good on your promise.

HERE'S HOW: Place your pointer finger sideways under your friend's nose and keep your arm straight and stiff. It's a very delicate spot and unless your friend is a great deal stronger than you are, you'll win the bet.

81 Knuckle Under

Touch the fingertips of your left hand to the fingertips of your right hand. Bend your middle fingers in half and place them so that both middle-finger knuckles are touching (see the picture).

You must keep your knuckles together.

You'll find that you can separate your thumbs without pulling the knuckles apart—and that you can separate your pointer fingers and your pinkies, but it is impossible (if you keep your knuckles touching) to separate your ring fingers.

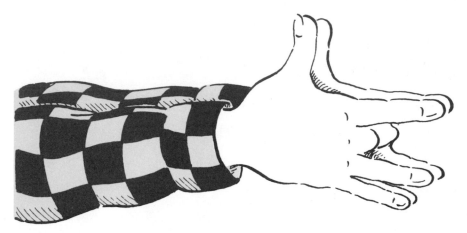

Here's another way to do the same "impossible." Have a friend place his or her hand so that the fingertips are *on the table,* with the middle finger tucked under. Then say, "You can lift your pinky without lifting that knuckle—you can raise your thumb—you can wiggle your pointer finger—but your ring finger is very heavy, isn't it? Try to lift it. Doesn't it feel like it weighs a ton?"

All people who are double-jointed: Disregard these two tricks! They'll be too easy for you!

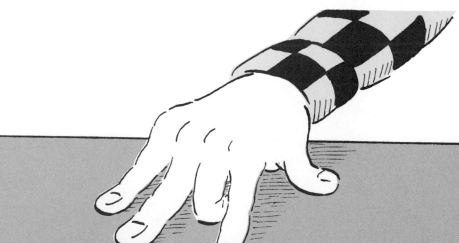

82 Super Stumpers

Here are some extra-tricky riddles to try out on friends:

Lying there in the yard so neat,
Something very good to eat.
It had neither flesh nor bone,
But in 21 days it walked alone.
What is it?

ANSWER: An egg.

What state is high in the middle and round at both ends?

ANSWER: oHIo.

What word is always pronounced wrong?

ANSWER: "Wrong"!

You don't have to be very good at math to figure out this stunt. How much dirt is there in a hole a foot long, a foot wide, and a foot deep?
Give up?

ANSWER: No matter how long, wide, or deep it is, there's no dirt in a hole!

STICKY SIDE

STICKY SIDE

STICKY SIDE

83 Presto Chango!

Turn a quarter into a dime, right before your friends' eyes. Now that's inflation for you!

Your audience sees a quarter on a table before them. Next you take a deck of cards, still in the package, and place the pack over the quarter. Suddenly you slap the top of the pack, lift it up, and the quarter has changed to a dime!

HERE'S HOW: Before you perform this trick, stick double-faced tape onto the back of the pack of cards. If you don't have double-faced tape, you can make a circle of regular tape, with the sticky side facing *out.* The picture shows you how.

NOW WATCH THIS!

On the tabletop, you hide a dime under the quarter. When you place the pack of cards on top of the quarter and slap it, the quarter sticks to the tape. After you lift up the pack of cards—making sure that the quarter is facing you and hidden from the audience—all that remains is the dime!

By the way—if possible, cover the table with a tablecloth before doing this trick.

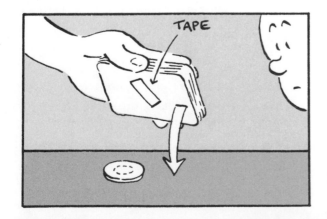

TAPE

84 Circle of Words

Draw a circle. (You can use the mouth of a cup to make the circle, or use a soup bowl if you want to play with a lot of words.)

Around the outside of the circle, print a word. Look at the last letter. Now think of another word—one that starts with the same letter. (So if you start with the word "top," you might follow it with "pat.")

And that's what you do, all around the circle. You print one word after another, with the last letter of each word being the same as the first letter of the next.

ONLY ONE RULE: You must go all around the circle without using any word twice!

85 Bull's-eye!

Your house is full of games you didn't know you owned—you just have to know where to find them!

Do you have a cotton swab? A drinking straw? A stub of a pencil, or a pen? Good! You have the makings of a fun game:

Make a circle out of your thumb and pointer finger. Lay a cotton swab or a half of a drinking straw across that circle.

The aim of the game is this: Using only that one hand, gently toss the stick into the air, and as it comes down, get it to go through the circle of your fingers. Once you get the knack of it, you can do it time after time.

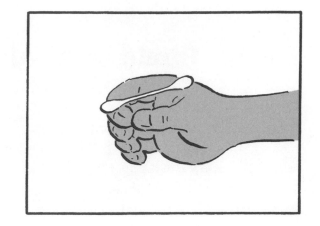

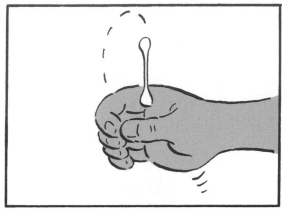

SHE'S THE **CHAMP!**

86 Sum Trick

All you need for this terrific trick is five scraps of paper.

On the first slip of paper, write a number 1 on the front and a 2 on the back. On the next piece of paper, scribble number 3 on one side, 4 on the other. Put a 5 and a 6 on the third scrap; a 7 and an 8 on the fourth; and a 9 and a 10 on the fifth scrap.

Then hand your friend all five pieces of paper, turn your back, and say, "Shuffle them, mix 'em up, turn 'em around, and then lay them out any way you want on the table.

"Now," you continue, with your back still to your friend, "tell me how many *odd* numbers are showing." As soon as your pal says how many odd numbers are face up, you'll be able to tell the sum of *all* the numbers showing!

HERE'S HOW: The sum of all the *even* numbers on the five pieces of paper is 30. All you have to do is subtract from 30 the *number* of odd numbers you're told are showing. For example, if 2 odd numbers are showing, take 2 away from 30, and announce that the sum of the numbers showing is 28. If your pal tells you that there are 4 odd numbers showing, you just subtract 4 from 30, and declare that the sum of the numbers in view is 26. Easy math, and I promise, it works every time.

P.S. Be sure to mark a little line under both the 6 and the 9—6 and 9. This way those two numbers can't get confused when you're playing out the trick.

NOW TELL ME HOW MANY **ODD** NUMBERS ARE SHOWING!

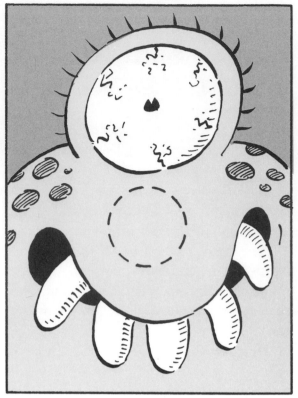

EEK!

87 Minimask

Are you tired of tripping as you go trick-or-treating because your mask is covering your eyes? Then a minimask is for you!

HERE'S HOW: Start with a square of paper about 3 inches on each side. Draw eyes along the top edge and a big mouth near the bottom; for a nose, draw a circle that is about the size of a nickel. Cut out enough of the center area of the circle so that you can fit this minimask securely onto your nose.

And that's it!

88 Buck in a Book

Put a dollar bill in a book and balance the book on end. Next, with your hands behind your back, stand on one foot and lean forward. The object is to try to pick the dollar bill out of the book with your teeth.

If you can get it, you can keep it—but until you actually *do* get it, don't bank on it.

89 The Almighty Dollar

You say, "I'll bet I can fix a dollar bill so that it will be absolutely impossible to tear in the middle." Your friends will probably say, "Oh, sure!" until you show them.

HERE'S WHAT YOU DO: Start rolling the bill from one of the corners, until the bill is tightly wound up in a compact roll. Then it's impossible to tear! (Well, maybe a circus strongman could tear it, but I can't, and I'll bet you can't either.)

90 Pete and Repeat

This gag is very old and will probably only work on people who are younger than you are. It's a story. You say, "There were two brothers, Pete and Repeat. Pete and Repeat went down the river in a boat. Pete fell out. Who was left?"

Now, if your friend was really listening, he will answer, "Repeat." At which point you *do* repeat the story, saying, "There were two brothers, Pete and Repeat. Pete and Repeat went down the river in a boat. Pete fell out. Who was left?"

And you keep it up until your friend realizes what a dumb joke you suckered him into.

91 Magic 37

I cannot believe what I'm going to tell you. I don't understand it either. I only know that this trick works every time.

Pick a number from 1 through 9 and multiply it by 3. Then divide the number you have now into the original number placed next to itself three times. I can promise you this: The answer is always 37.

For example, say you pick the number 4. Four times 3 is 12. Now divide 12 into 444 and you get 37.

Or let's say you pick 2. Two times 3 is 6. Divide 6 into 222 and—surprise, surprise—you'll get 37.

If you prefer, take 5. Five times 3 is 15. Divide 15 into 555 and—guess what?—you get 37 again.

I know a number of number tricks, but I number this number trick number one!

92 In One Breath

Try saying to your friends, "In the next 30 seconds, can you name Disney's seven dwarfs?" They'll miss a couple—I guarantee it! How many can *you* name? They are Sleepy, Sneezy, Doc, Dopey, Grumpy, Happy, and Bashful.

In one breath, can you and your friends name eight parts of the body that are spelled with three letters? I'll start you off with "arm." And remember, slang words don't count—just real words.

ANSWER: eye, ear, arm, leg, rib, toe, hip, lip.

93 Can You Topple This?

The point of this game is to take turns building a toothpick tower until it topples.

On a tabletop, place two toothpicks one way, then two toothpicks the other way (across the first two), and so on, counting toothpicks as you go.

The player who adds on the last two toothpicks without toppling over the tower is the winner.

94 No, Not That Way

If you're going to pull a smart-alecky stunt on a friend, it's a good idea to quickly follow it with an interesting one. That way, you can keep your friend as a *friend.* Here's a smart-alecky "betcha." And after that, I'll tell you an interesting one:

Say to your pal, "I bet I can make you open your eyes. First *close* your eyes." And as soon as your friend closes his or her eyes, you say, "No, not that way!" Your pal will open both eyes to see how it *should* be done. Then you say, "See, I made you open your eyes!"

Now, instead of ducking, you immediately say, "No, seriously—here's a real good stunt." And then do the next trick for your pal.

95 Touch the Tips!

Close your eyes. Stretch your arms out to the side. Point your pointer fingers in toward your center. Bend your elbows a lot, and bring your fingertips together without opening your eyes. Do it quickly. Oddly enough, it's almost impossible. Oh, it's not *impossibly* impossible. I mean, you'll be able to touch your fingertips together every once in a while. But not very often.

96 Four from Four

Is it possible to take 4 away from 4 and be left with 8?

Yes!

HERE'S HOW: Start with a square piece of paper. Cut off the four corners as shown. You'll end up with eight corners!

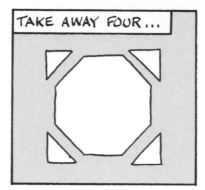

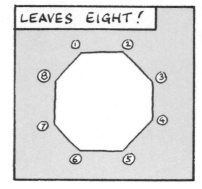

97 Jack Can't Jump over the Candlestick

You hold up a small object—a penny, pencil, wallet, or whatever—and say, "I'll bet that I can put this on the floor in such a way that absolutely no one can jump over it. Is it a bet?" And when your friend agrees, you just put the object on the floor, touching the wall.

Can't jump over that, can you?

98 Fold It Up

Give your friend a sheet of newspaper and say, "I bet you can't fold the paper in half eight times, because it can't be done." And no matter how hard your pal tries, the eighth fold will be impossible to make.

If you want to try this with a dollar bill, you'll be surprised to find that you can only fold it in half six times. In order to make that seventh fold, you'd have to put the bill in a vise.

99 The Force

A real magician can force you to pick the card he or she wishes without your ever knowing that you're being forced at all. Here's a whiz of a way to "force" a card.

Before you perform this trick, secretly choose whatever card you want your pal to pick and put it on top of the deck. Then put two cards on top of it. *You are going to force your friend to choose the third card in the deck.*

When you do the trick, deal the top six cards of the deck face down onto a table, *laying them down from your left to your right.* The card you will force your friend to pick is now third from the left.

Then you say to your friend, "I know which of these cards you're going to choose. In fact, I'm now writing down the name of that card." And you do. "I'm folding up the paper." You do that, too. "And I'm putting it aside until later.

"Now," you say, "tell me any number from one to six."

If your friend picks "one," you start from the left and spell out "O-N-E," tapping one card as you say each letter. You will land on the correct card. Turn it over.

If your friend picks "two," do the same thing, spelling and tapping from the left, "T-W-O."

If your pal chooses "three," simply say, "One, two, three," still counting and tapping from the left. Again you'll land on the third card—the one you wrote down.

Here's the sneaky part—if "four" is picked, spell and tap from the *right* end, "F-O-U-R," which makes you land on that same third card from the left.

If "five" is selected, also spell from the right, "F-I-V-E."

But if your friend says "six," just spell from the left again, "S-I-X."

As soon as you've landed on the card and have turned it over, show your pal the slip of paper on which you named that same card. There's the living proof of what a mind reader you are!

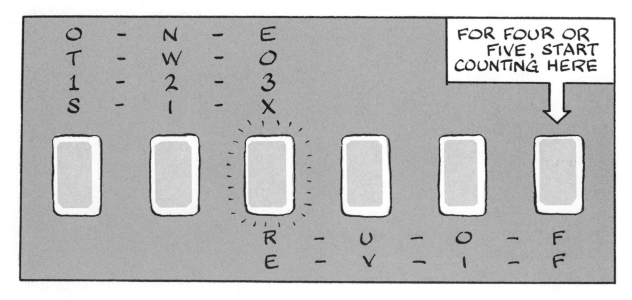

88

100 **Baseball Mystery**

Can you solve this mystery?

You have a baseball. You throw it away from you as hard as you can. It doesn't hit anything, nor does anybody catch it, but it comes back to you. There are no strings or elastics involved. Why does the ball come back?

Give up?

Because you threw it up instead of backward or forward.

101 Double Your Money

How'd you like to crumple a single dollar bill into a ball, rub it on your elbow for luck, and have it turn into two bills? You can!

HERE'S HOW: A second dollar bill, wadded into a ball, is secretly wedged between your shirt collar and the back of your neck (picture 1).

When you're ready to do the trick, show the first dollar bill to your audience. Crumple it into a ball and hold it between the tips of your left fingers and thumb. Say that you have to rub it on your elbow for luck. Bend your right arm. As you rub the bill on your right elbow the fingers of your right hand secretly steal the hidden bill from your collar (picture 2).

Once you've got it, stop rubbing your elbow. Look at the first bill closely. Say that it looks as though you didn't rub it enough. Lower your right arm and put the first bill in your right fist. (Now your right fist is holding two bills.) Bend your left arm and, in the same way, rub that elbow with the bills in your right fist (picture 3).

Bring your hands together, grasp a bill between the fingertips of each hand, and pull your hands apart as though you were tearing a bill in two (picture 4). Roll each one in your fingers for a second or two and then drop the bills separately on the table. Open them up, smooth them out, and put them away in your wallet as you smile and say, "What a way to double your money!"

Practice this trick by performing it for your dog before you try it on real live people.